In The Joy of Christ

Robert S. Howard M.D.

THANK YOU FOR THE MORNING LIGHT

PRAYERS FOR CHILDREN

RECEIVED AND ILLUSTRATED BY
ROBERT SWAIM FLOWERS

ISBN-10: 1942526237
ISBN-13: 978-1942526230

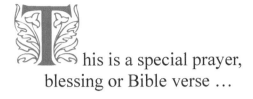

his is a special prayer,
blessing or Bible verse …

for

_____

…to whom this book is given.

_____

_____

_____

_____

_____

From _____

Amen

DEDICATION

For my sons
Swaim, Rob, Christian and Jonathan
who were raised with my prayers,
and to my precious wife Susan,
who was an answer to my prayers.

ACKNOWLEDGEMENTS

This is your gift LORD-
Thank you for the pleasure and delight of creating verse and getting lost
in the simple wonder of paint, colored pencils and paper.

To my beloved wife Susan - my muse, my joy and my prayer partner.
I am so grateful that she understands my need to disappear into the
heavenly realm of poetry and art.

To our earth angel, Edie Hand. You are woven into the fabric of our
family; without you this prayer book would not have finally taken wing.

And to the dream team of Wanda McKoy, Peggy Jones,
Diane Penney and Mark Dubis — a thousand thanks.

FOREWORD

These prayers were inspired by an immigrant friend who requested bedtime prayers in English for her young daughter. I tried, but my several attempts were unsatisfactory. But not long thereafter my wife and I had our own little ones and I felt a unique urge for prayers for small children. This time I went to God asking His help. What began as "Stay the Night Beside My Bed," had soon grown into a collection of 80+ prayers by the time our boys finished grade school.

My wife Susan and I cherished and memorized many of these prayers, as did our two young sons. But many were special for our adult needs. We particularly enjoyed reciting the prayers in "alternating phrase" interplay. This was something the whole family came to enjoy, which lifted us all in togetherness with God – each morning and evening, and often at differing times during each day.

You will find prayers suitable for most all occasions and situations, from special joys to stage fright, and from furry friends, to fear of the dark, and many more. Your children will learn that there is nothing too small or too great for God's Glory and His sharing. These simple prayers are both for our children, and for us as parents – a continuity of Grace especially helpful during these challenging growth years of family life.

These prayers from their inception have been genuine gestures of worship and gratitude – a tribute to the beauty of life, the awesomeness of God, the presence of the Holy Spirit, and the Grace of our Lord Jesus Christ. They are meant to be used, and reused. And typically that is what happens, for children inherently love rhyme, memorization, and repetition – especially when combined with alternating the phrases in an intimate loving ritual. Both we, and our children, loved interposing the recited prayers with memorized scripture, like the 23rd Psalm, plus free flowing thanksgiving, prayerful petitions, and Godly conversation.

Although original, the prayers within are far from my own. They are rather God's gift through me, often arriving late at night or in the early morning hours. Other prayers came in the midst of the hustle and bustle while passing through an ordinary day, sometimes even while coaching little league baseball.

The book is filled with love, joy, gratitude, and with God's Grace. Invite it into your life and be blessed.

Robert S. Flowers, MD

CONTENTS

MORNING LIGHT

Dear God,

Thank You for the morning light,
That You were with me through the night.
Thank you for this brand new day,
For life and health . . . for books, for play!

Make today especially good
And help me do the things I should.
At home, at work, at play, at school,
Let me live the golden rule . . .

. . . And treat each person that I see
Like I would choose that they treat me.

Amen.

DON'T FORGET MY NAME

Dear God,

Stay the night
Beside my bed,
And choose the thoughts
Within my head.
Take away
All fear and shame,
And don't forget,
Dear God, my name,
" _____ _____ ".

Amen.

After this prayer my sons and I always pray, "Lord, we know
You will never forget us, but help us also, we pray, not to forget
You as we go through each day!"

THAT I SHOULD LOVE
(The Great Commandment)*

Dear God,

That "*I should love*", is Your Command**
"*The Lord my God*", and You demand . . .
"*With all my heart, and strength and soul*" —
"*And love my neighbor*" — that's my goal. ***

Those words are big and I'm not sure
If I know how to love that pure.
So let me start with love I know,
And make it stronger as I grow

Amen.

* Matthew 22:36-40
** Deuteronomy 6:4-9
*** Leviticus 19:18

MUSIC

Thank you, God,

or songs to sing
For notes to play
And bells to ring
For strings to pluck
For horns to toot
They're much more fun
Than guns to shoot
For iphones, ipods,
And radio
I'm happy, Lord,
You let me know . . .

The joy of music!

Amen.

TO GLORIFY GOD

Lord,

It's a great big word, to "Glorify" –
I don't fully "get it", but still I try!
It somehow means … to honor You …
In all the things I say and do.

To put You first … in everything –
First in my heart, and the songs I sing!
For the "Glorify You" is my life's main chore,
And to enjoy You forever … and forever more!

Amen.

From Westminster Confession – (for children).

SPECIAL JOYS

Thank you, God,

For trees to climb
And words that rhyme
For pools to splash
And clay to mash
For frozen ponds
And snowy fronds
For piles of leaves
And Christmas Eves
For balls to kick
And berries to pick
For summer ways
On sunny days
For ice cream cones
And jelly scones
For open space. . .
And Godly grace.

Amen.

WITH ALL MY HEART

R. Flowers.
© 2008

MORE LIKE JESUS

Every day Lord,
Help me be
More like Jesus,
Set me free;

Teach me, please,
The perfect art
Of loving You
With all my heart!

Amen.

A LITTLE BIT OF GOD

Creator God, you gave to me –
A wondrous gift, and it's all free!
You let me sing and make up songs,
And find out ways to undo wrongs.

You let me draw and gave me paint,
To use with brush without constraint.
You taught my hands to work with clay,
And let me make things everyday.

Creative love, the love to create –
It's Yours,…now mine, and I can't wait!

Thank you, Creator God.

Amen.

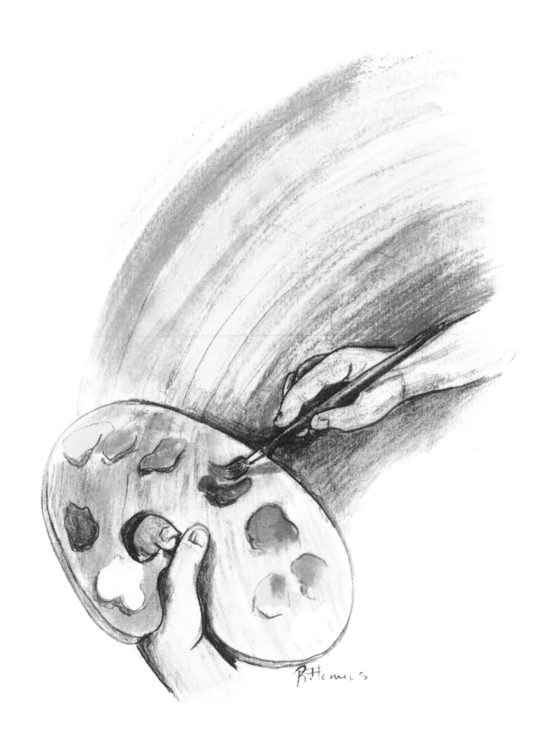

COLORS

Dear God,

For red and orange
And sunset stuff,
As if purple skies
Were not enough!

For mist and rainbows
And gray-green hills,
For maple leaves
And autumn thrills,

For silver clouds
And golden rays,
We give you thanks
And send you praise.

Amen.

BLESSING FOR ONE

Thank you, God,
For food and drink,
For songs to sing,
And thoughts to think –
For field and forest,
Sky and sea,
And thank you, God,
For loving me.

Amen.

R. Flowers
©2008

BLESSING AT MEALTIME

Dear God,

All the world
Belongs to You –
The earth, the sky
The ocean blue;

And we are Yours,
And what we do,
So bless this meal,
And bless us too!

Amen.

BE MY LIGHT

Dear God,

Beside my bed
I kneel and pray
That You will come
Close by and stay,
And be my Light
To show the way…
To Godly love
And Godly play!

Amen.

YOUR SEA'S SO GREAT

O God, please wait,
Or I might fall.
Your sea's so great,
And my boat's so small.

Amen.

R. Flowers

ANOINT ME LORD

Rain on me, Lord,
With your Holy Spirit —
So when you speak.
I clearly hear it.

Anoint me, Lord
With gifts and power —
So I, just as a child,
This very hour...

Claim the promise
That I know is real —
Your gift to bless,
Forgive and heal!

Amen.

FOLLOW THE LEADER

Jesus, Savior,

Take my hand.
  Lead me down
The path You planned.

And if the path
Has holes or boulders,
Just lift me up
On Your big shoulders

Thank you,
Lord,
Amen.

A CHILD OF GRACE

God above,
Come be with me,
Send Your love,
And help me be
A child of grace –
All pure within,
Free from pride
From fear, from sin!

Amen.

48

36

12

R. Flowers
© 2008

STRONG AND TALL

Lord, You see,
I'm very small.
I'd like to be
Both strong and tall.
Give me Grace,
And keep me pure.
Until my faith,
Is full and sure.

Amen.

FOR MOM

Dear God,

Help my mom
Throughout the day—
She spends her time
To ease my way.

Give her love
And time to rest,
And keep her safe
For she's the best . . .

. . . Mom in the whole world.

Amen.

IN YOUR LIGHT

Lord, let your spirit fall on me.
And show me the "stuff" I need to see –
That clutter hidden deep inside
That I try to ignore, but for which you died!

Let me see . . . but not be afraid,
'Cause on your cross my debt was paid.
Forgiving so much, and loving so grand –
Now and forever I just want to stand . . .

In your light . . .

Composed . . . by my youthful son, Christian,
with a few words changed to "rhyme" . . . by his dad.

45

MAKEUP

Dear God,

I can do make-up
And change my looks,
And pretend I'm a person
I read of in books;

But You, Lord, alone,
Creator and Teacher—
Can make me, in Christ,
A completely new creature!

Amen.

REMEMBER ME

Dear Lord, You know
Each grain of sand
And all the lines
That crease my hand.

And every night
When I'm in bed
You know each thought
Inside my head.

And since You know
What I would say,
Remember me,
When I don't pray!

Amen.

GLOBAL PRAYER

Dear God,

Bless the children 'round the world;
North, East, South, and West.
Fill their stomachs, fill their hearts,
And keep them while they rest.

Amen.

R. Flowers
© 1993

DEPLOYED PARENT

Dear God,

My Dad's deployed
Across the Sea,
Protecting our Country
Keeping it free!

I know he's in danger,
But he's not alone –
You're there to protect him,
You love him as Your own.

He's the key to our family,
We miss him so much!
So bring him back safe –
To love, care and touch.

Thank you, Lord
Amen.

MY CONFESSION

Lord God,

Some precious words* You said to pray
When we arise – then late each day –
When we lie down, before we sleep.
It's like a trust I vow to keep.

*"I will love the Lord my God
With all my heart, wherever I trod,
With all my soul and all my might"* . . .
I'll pray this prayer, . . . both day and night.

And You will make the rains to fall**
So grass is green and grain grows tall,
And olives swell, and grapes grow sweet
And there's good food for us to eat.

Dear Lord, this prayer, I promise now,
Will bind my wrists and touch my brow.
It's on my door and gate so styled***
That all will know that I'm Your child.

Amen.

* Deuteronomy 6:4-9 (Shema for, "Hear, O Israel")
** Deuteronomy 6:5
*** Deuteronomy 11:14-15

BATHING A BABY

Dear God,

Bless this life
Now soaking wet
Who absolutely
Loves to get
Bathed in water,
From toes to face —
Cleansed by God
And filled with Grace!

Amen.

A PRAYER AFTER EATING
("BURPING PRAYER")[*]

Dear God,

This is a prayer for a full little baby,
That You help with his[*] bubble, and then perhaps, maybe,
After he burps he'll fall off to sleep,
And then, precious Lord, I pray You will keep . . .

This wee little creature safe from all harm.
Surround him and shield him with Your big loving arm.
Help him to grow in the right sort of ways,
And be there for "bubbles" the rest of his days.

Amen.

[*]This prayer, when memorized by new parents, adds strength and comfort during unrelenting hours of infant care. It invokes God's presence in the most basic of life's tasks, "burping" a baby. Often parents recite it hundreds of times in the course of caring for each infant. The prayer invokes God's special presence for all future events which may befall this sweet new life.

BEFORE THE GAME

Dear God,

I know this game is just for fun
And it matters little when we're done –
Whether we win or whether we lose,
But give me strength so I can choose
To give the best I have in me . . .
. . . To help us win, if that can be!

Amen.

Amen!

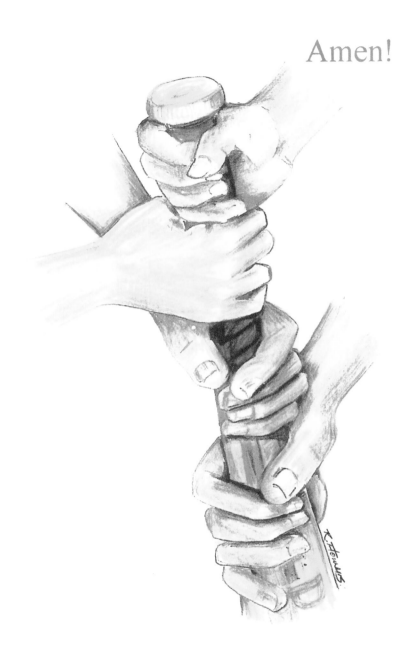

Play Ball!

A GOOD SPORT

Help us God, to play our best
Whenever our team is put to the test
Help us not to push or shove,
In all our play, Lord, teach us love…
… And always help me be a good sport!

Amen.

Sheldon   R. Flowers

BITS OF HEAVEN

Dear Lord, You design
Such wonderful things –
Each creature You make,
And each bird that sings –

I love Your starfish,
Sea shells and surprises –
All bits of heaven
In earthly disguises!

Thank You,
Precious Lord
Amen.

EARTH PRAYER

Help us, Lord, to see the earth
As a garden we must tend –
The forests, streams, the air, the sea –
On these our lives depend!

Help us know each bird and fish
And every beast as friend,
And that . . . if we hurt the world You made,
It hurts us in the end!

Amen.

STILL THE STORM

Lord Jesus,

Still the sea
And calm the wind—
Just say the word,
The *storm* will end.

You did it once
In Galilee.
Please do it again
When the *storm's* in me.

Amen.

THE SAND AND WATER

O God,

The water's deep,
And I'm not tall.
Your ocean's immense,
And I'm so small.

So stay close by,
And hold my hand –
When my feet are in water,
And my toes touch the sand.

Amen.

OTHERS NEAR AND FAR

Dear God,

Today I pray
For those I love.
Please send them help
From heaven above;

And those whose names
Seem just a word,
Those unknown "ones" –
Of whom I've heard.

And I pray for people
I've never met . . .
If they're cold
Or hungry, or wet . . .

Then clothe them, feed them,
Hold them tight,
And surround them with
Your love tonight.

Amen.

DIFFERENT

ord,
You made me different
From others I've met,
Which means I'm special,
And I can't forget!

It also means
You trust me most
To give me this challenge*
Others can't boast.

Amen.

*Substitute: gift, talent, problem,
burden, etc.

WHEN PARENTS FIGHT

I don't know why,
Dear God, they fuss –
My mom and dad,
When it's just us.

Please help them see
Your love's enough
To help them stop
Their hurtful stuff.

Amen.

74

PRAYER FOR SOMEONE YOU DON'T LIKE

I t's a hard, hard task
To say this prayer—
But You said, "Ask",
So I guess I dare . . .

. . . To forgive and bless
_____, who doesn't act nice.
Since this prayer's so hard . . .
Please bless him/her twice!

Amen.

HELP DAD UNDERSTAND

Dear God,

Please help my dad
To understand
When things don't go
The way he planned . . .

He's disappointed.
We both feel bad,
Help him forgive –
To stop being mad!

Touch his heart
So he can say,
"You're just learning.
That's okay!"

Amen.

BIRTHDAY TOMORROW

Dear God,

Tomorrow's very special
It's the day that I was born
And I'll be one year older
Early in the morn.

Throughout this coming year
Increase the things I know
And help me get much wiser
With each inch I grow.

So please be at my party.
And linger after it's ended,
And I'll remember always
The birthday God attended!

                        Amen.

THANKSGIVING PRAYER

Dear God,

Birds sing songs,
And we give praise –
That You provide
For all our days.

With Love and Grace –
Both always there,
And food and drink –
Enough to share!

And for loving care
That fills our shelves . . .
We give You back,
In thanks, ourselves!

Amen.

ADVENT

God, I watched
A candle lighted
For Advent Season.
I'm excited!

It's hope for good
When all seems bad,
For God was born
To make us glad.

Bells inside
Us girls and boys
Ring a bright
And Holy noise

They chime a song,
Called "Peace on Earth,
Goodwill to All":
It's Jesus' birth!

Amen.

A NEW BABY

Soon, Dear God, there'll be another,
A baby sister or a brother!
I'll need Your help to learn to share,
And give Mom time for "Baby's" care.

Prepare my heart to love this one
Who'll be too small to crawl or run;
Keep Mom strong through baby's birth
So our sweet home can bless the earth!

Amen.

CHRISTMAS STAR

Dear God,

Thank You for
That shining light –
That Christ our King
Was born this night.

For peace on earth,
Good will toward men –
That we are free
From all our sin

But God, . . . You know,
So much has changed!
My little heart . . .
Is rearranged.

For just because
That baby came . . .
My life will never
Be the same.

Thank You, God.

Amen.

CHRISTMAS JOYS

Dear God,

For Christmas Eve
And the Gospel we believe,
For trees we trim
To remind us of Him,
For gifts to wrap
And holiday naps,
For presents to shake
That we hope don't break,
For ice skates that fit…
And night ponds well lit!
And sledding down hills
With thrills and spills,

For snowmen and angels
We make out of snow,
And piles of snowballs
To gather and throw!
For twinkling lights
And "shiny brights",
For Carols to sing
And bells to ring,
For Christmas treats
And good things to eat!
For Jesus' birth –
And hope on Earth,
For stars in space…
And saving Grace

We thank You, God.

                    Amen.

ON STAGE

Dear God,

feel afraid
Out there on stage
It's awfully big
When you're my age.

Just help me please,
To do my best,
I'll let You handle
All the rest.

Amen.

SPEECH FRIGHT

Dear God,

 feel so small,
And want to run
I wish this speech
Were already done!

So make me calm
And sure, I ask,
So I'm at my best
To do this task.

                     Amen.

TWO TIMES

Dear God, I know
I should be nice,
But today I failed,
I did it twice.

So please forgive
And clear my heart –
So I can make
A fresh new start.

Amen.

GOOD FRIDAY

Dear God,

This is Good Friday
The day that You died
But I know You are living —
You're with me inside.

They say in Your dying
That death simply shatters —
And in it You teach us
That it's Christ's Love that matters!

Amen.

RESURRECTION

Dear God,

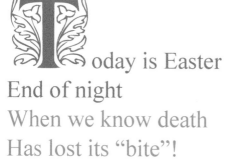oday is Easter
End of night
When we know death
Has lost its "bite"!

As morning breaks
Heal all our pain.
Good-bye to sadness...
Let joy reign!

But, baby bunnies?
And eggs dyed bright?
And fresh hatched chickens?
Bless their sight!

They're New Life signs
This Easter Morn,
Which is why on Christmas
Christ was born!

RESURRECTION!

                    Amen.

LOSS OF A PET

Dear God,

This is _____,
And now that You've met
Please adopt my friend,
Care for my pet.

When dear ones depart
It hurts, You know.
So mend my heart
As days come and go.

                        Amen.

FURRY FRIENDS

Thank You, God, for my furry friend,
Who tells the truth and won't pretend.
He licks my face to say "hello",
And comes along wherever I go.

He makes me smile when I feel sad,
And loves me when I'm acting bad.
I know he'll stick by to the end,
So thank You for my furry friend!

Amen.

WHEN MOM DOESN'T HAVE TIME

Dear God,

In case my mom
Won't stop to pray
I'll try to tell you
Things she'd say.

***

"Please bless this home
And all herein
And bless each task
That we begin".

"And forgive my words
That sound unkind
They're not the ones
I had in mind."

"Give us food
To grace our table.
Make me strong
When I'm not able".

"Bless our kin
And all who're sick,
And all the friends
You helped us pick".

"Remind me often
To pause and pray,
And renew my faith
For every day".

***

This is stuff
My Mom would say
If she had time
To praise and pray.

So grant her needs
Be they old or new.
As she, in silence –
Talks to You!

Amen.

PARENT'S PRAYER
FOR A CRANKY INFANT

God, In Your wisdom
Help me to cope
With this wild cranky baby
Who's just teething, I hope . . .

Or hungry, or sleepy,
Or maybe just tired,
Or perhaps his/her sweet system
Has simply misfired.

Give me the patience
To parent this child,
And please heal what's making
My baby so wild.

                              Amen.

A NEW DAD'S PRAYER

Help me, Lord, to be a good father
And go a step beyond.
May diapers and burps never be a bother,
But just a chance to bond!

Thank you, God.

Amen.

MY CHILD IS SICK

Lord,

Here I hold our precious child,
So hot, so very ill
In Jesus' name let him* be healed
And let that be Your will.

Rain down upon him, Holy Spirit
Put joy upon his face,
Restore him by Your power, Lord,
And by Your awesome Grace!

Amen.

*Substitute feminine for masculine when appropriate.

MY CHILD IS WELL

Dear God,

My child, so sick,
Has turned around
The fever's gone
New health is found.

Through all those days
I feared the worst
But You stayed close
As doctor-nurse.

So thank You, Lord.
For life's new lease –
Your gift of Joy,
Of Health and Peace.

Amen.

GOD'S LIGHT

Dear Lord,

Here in the dark
I'm wide awake,
I fear night stuff,
And wait daybreak.

Here in the dark
I feel alone,
So send me Your light,
I'll make it my own!

Amen.

SCARY THINGS

Dear God,

I fear the dark and hidden stuff,
And wish I were tall and strong and tough.
I know that monsters don't exist
But at night they're on my "scary list".

So when I have a frightful thought,
Bring back to me the words You taught,
Like – "Let the children come unto me",
And "wherever You are, there I'll be".

Thank You, Jesus
Amen.

"NIGHT" IN ARMOR

Dear God,

Come stay within
My heart tonight,
And take away
All fear and fright.

To keep me safe
You gave me Your "nod"
And dubbed me a "knight"
With the whole armor of God!

Amen.

*Ephesians 6:11-18
The Belt of Truth
The Breastplate of Righteousness
Swift Shoes as the Gospel of Peace
The Helmut of Salvation
The Shield of Faith
The Sword of the Spirit – the Word of God

THROUGHOUT THE NIGHT

Father, take
My fears away,
And keep me safe
'Til break of day.
Be like my dad,
And stay nearby.
To hold me close,
So I won't cry.

Amen.

R. Flowers
© 2009

GOODNIGHT, DEAR LORD

Goodnight, Dear Lord,
I close my eyes
Within Your arms
Where no child cries.

There's no more need
To think or do,
So Goodnight, Lord,
I rest with You.

                                   Amen.

ABOUT THE AUTHOR

Robert S. Flowers, MD is an internationally renown plastic surgeon.
After 40 years in the Hawaiian Islands he moved back home to
the red clay of Alabama. He lives with his wife Susan in a
ridge-top home God has blessed as a sanctuary and gathering place
for children of all ages.

CPSIA information can be obtained at www.ICGtesting.com
Printed in the USA
LVOW01*1258140415

433006LV00003BA/3/P

9 781942 526230